AWAKENED
BY MY

Angels

LEARNING TO HEAL

MAXINE ALLEN RIFENBURGH

BALBOA.
PRESS

A DIVISION OF HAY HOUSE

Balboa Press books may be ordered through booksellers or by contacting:

Balboa Press
A Division of Hay House
1663 Liberty Drive
Bloomington, IN 47403
www.balboapress.com
1 (877) 407-4847

Print information available on the last page.

ISBN: 978-1-5043-7129-2 (sc)
ISBN: 978-1-5043-7144-5 (e)

Balboa Press rev. date: 12/30/2016

Dedicated my children

Sweet Boy and Angel Baby
I would not have re-found my inner self and strength
without you two being my driving force.
And
to my Family of Angels
Daddy
My Grandparents
My Great Grandparents
My Great Great Grandparents
My Uncles and my Baby Brother
All whom have passed over

I started on my journey 12 years ago, little did I know that it was a journey that I had been on since I was a child. 11 years ago, I divorced after a 24-year marriage. No one even had any idea that for the entirety of my marriage there was domestic violence. I never told a soul. I just kept saying I can make it better. It is what we do when confronted daily with domestic violence. I did not want anyone to know. Especially my family. I made my choice and they would say, or at least I thought, you made your bed, you lie in it.

With that all said, I made a vow to myself that I would help others anyway I could. With my career in retail, I could touch a few lives. My work kept me busy so I struggled to find the time was the excuse I made to myself. My career gave me protection in my travels during the week. I traveled over the Northwest with 4 different companies. Staying in a hotel was safety for me and it kept my children from seeing me abused. This book is comprised of poems I wrote over the last 5 years, 7 years after my divorce to help me heal.

Something that needs to be said at the beginning of this book. I've had dreams for many years that told me of my future. For example: I knew I would marry my husband when I met him. He was the groom in my dream I had at age 16. I met him at 17 at a wedding. He was one of the groom's men and I was the maid of honor. The bride had been trying to get me to meet him for close to a year. But, I knew that my mom and stepdad would not have approved of me dating him. After the wedding, he asked me out. There was no keeping me from accepting his offer to go to a movie. Two years later we married.

I knew when he had his first affair. I was on the front lawn of our little rental house a week prior. The message I received was simply. "He is seeing someone else". That was on a Sunday. I pushed the message and my feeling down inside thinking "he loves me, It's my imagination." On Friday evening I was working at one my store locations. I had the feeling or urge to call home. I went out into the mall's main walkway. Picked up the pay phone. When he answered, I asked "Who the hell is she?" I just knew. He told me he was involved with a woman who was older than him, and they were planning on going away in the morning for a weekend together. She was a receptionist at his companies' office. He did not know if he wanted to stay married. He needed to go away with her to see what he wanted. I drove home, cried the whole way. I knew there was no changing his mind. One of the most heart wrenching experiences of my life. Watching her pull up in her car the next morning out front of our little home, and the 2 of them driving away together.

We'd been married for almost 7 years and I stayed for another 17 years. I turned off or tuned out my angels. Or intuition during this period. I went into survival mode. It took a painful year for my divorce to be final and for another 4 years I tuned out. Yet I did write about my Domestic Violence period and shared with the people who touch my life during the court enforced DV classes. After my son started up where his dad had left off and I finally had the nerves to stand up for myself and my children. My love was too strong for them both for them to think they could repeat what they had learned.

So here it is:

It did not start as physical abuse. But, something much more subtle and dangerous. It was a word here and there telling me I wasn't good enough, enough, sexy enough. That I was cold, stupid, and ugly. I made him mad. I made him call me names like Cunt, Bitch, and Whore. If I did not make him mad he would not call me names, or spit on me.

I remember him calling me at work and screaming at me over the phone, because I had forgotten to write down a check in the checkbook. I remember him telling me, "If he did not get it at home, there were many women he worked with who would." There are other memories that I do not let myself think about.

After 7 years of marriage he had his first affair, "She" was the one who told him that she would give him love, that I must not love him. We separated, I watched him drive away while he decided if he wanted to stay with me. I called my sister up and she came and we packed up all the possessions from my marriage. I moved out for two months, went to counseling and then he asked me to come home. He did not need counseling it was my problems that caused our problems. That made him do and say all these horrible things. I believed him. I who wanted to be loved so desperately.

There were the good years. We had a son and then 5 years later a daughter. When she was 11 months old, He started to hit me. I did not call the police. I did not fight back. I cried and told him I was sorry that I made him angry. I lied to myself again and said it must have been me. I just need to try harder.

For the next 11 years, I tried, and tried and tried. I let him take my power, my dignity, and my respect. Not just my respect but also the respect of my children. The last two years of my marriage I would drive to work and rock in my driver's seat and chant just 6 more years, my daughter will be old enough in six more years. Then I can leave.

Then the day he put his hand around my neck and shook me like a rag doll. I realized that he could have killed me. I knew that six more years was not an option. That was in August of 2004. It took me till Easter Sunday of 2005 to walk out. I left my home, my children, my life and started on my new journey.

In January of 2006 the divorce was final. My daughter is still with her father and oldest, my son lives with me. He has started where his Dad left off. I'm called a bad parent, a whore Mom. That I need to apologize to his Father for leaving the family. My journey is now to heal my children and undo the poison that they saw growing up. I know it will not be easy. I know that this next year is all I have till my son becomes a man. That I have six months, to one year to teach, and show him that all people deserve respect. I may not reach my child, the damage of not leaving his father the first moment I was called a name may be too ingrained in my son. And that I may have to let him find his own path through his own years of abuse. But I must try for his sake.

As for my daughter, she is blossoming and each time I see her I cherish each moment. I am establishing with her a new identity. That I am worth loving and worth respecting. I ask from her, respect for me and for herself. She is only thirteen.

I will reach my goal to teach my children a different way of life and loving. This is my new life and journey. In many ways, it will be painful. But in the long run it will have been worth it. Half of my life is over, lived in the shadow of a monster call Domestic Violence. The shadow is gone; the monster has been slain and I will live in the sunlight and live each day to its fullest. Not just for me, but for my children.

Maxine

I was now on a new chapter of my life and journey. I was still blocked from my Angels or so I thought. I was with a good but misguided man for 4 years until I said no more. There is domestic violence that involves all physical, mental, verbal and financial abuse. I was a slow learner or choose not to listen to my Angels. This man took advantage of me financially and tried to control me. He would use my relationship with my son as his leverage.

After this period, I started reading books that were inspirational and about self-healing. More importantly I started to talk to God daily and renewed my faith in God. Because going to my therapist weekly was not helping me one iota. I could only take so much of my self-reflection and asking how did that make you feel. Made me feel like crap and for me just kept the cycle of DV alive. I am not saying that seeing a therapist is not needed. For me revisiting each week the trauma of Domestic Violence was too painful. I needed to reconnect to my inner self.

As I read and prayed I started to remember my dreams as a child. Knowing there was something in the closet at the home we lived in as a little child under the age of 5. Questioning who was there. At age 8, my night time visit from my Angel. I still see her as clearly today as I did that night. She glowed pure white light. She never said a word to me just passed by to let me know she was near. Spending time by myself in the forest and hills around my home as a child, was where I felt safe and content. I could talk to whoever was there and hear their replies in my head and feel them next to me. Slowly I was being made aware of my angels and renewing my faith in myself and in God.

My sister, brother and I were sleeping out on the deck of our home as we did many times during the summer. I remember clearly waking up in the night watching the stars as they glowed. I turned over onto my stomach, my head propped on my hands looking out over the yard towards the fields and woods. There she was in the little gully walking out of the woods and down the hill. This woman that just glowed white, her head tilted down as if in prayer. She did not look towards me, but I just felt peace. Not scared or concerned, total peace. I have this in my head like it was yesterday. Maybe she was there to let me know all would be okay. My parents had divorced the prior year. Life was traumatic and I had a new step-grandfather who liked little girls and boys in a way that I could not conceive yet.

Blessing's Bestowed

I saw an Angel when I was small
Her luminous light glowed in the night
She drifted down through the field
In that moment time stood still
I gazed upon her silently
Feeling small and scared to breathe

As I gazed upon her heavenly glow
A luminous light lit up the night.
And as she faded away from me
I felt her blessings bestowed to me

To help you understand my poetry, I need to begin with my family. My brother and sister are my closest allies. We were inseparable as kids. The three musketeers, and we gave our mother a bumpy ride and she taught us to laugh, sing and take whatever life had to offer in stride. Dad taught us to explore, love nature and be strong in heart and mind. My early childhood was magical, full of love and adventure.

This is my early childhood in a little sweet moment:

Three little Angels

Three little giggles in the breeze
Tinkling laughter through the trees
Little faces browned from the sun
Bare feet that hop skip and jump
Mischief lights up their eyes
As summer days' drift on by
Childhood memories I cherish most
Three little angels in a devil's cloak….

My first poem I wrote. It just came to me as they all do. I do not sit and say "Hey! I am going to write a poem about…" It does not work that way for me. My poetry is from my family who've passed over and my Angels who guide me. I refer to them as my Family of Angels. And my poems come my life experiences and the dreams I've had.

With this stated, I must mention Belle my great grandmother. My Daddy gifted me before he passed, her wedding ring. Inscribed on the inside is the dates she and Jack were engaged and married. I wear it so I can hear her clearly. I never knew Belle. She passed. 18 months before I was born. But I knew of her presence. The home my great grandfather built for her is still standing on the little slope above the stream next to my grandparents' home. When I was a child the path my grandfather made going from his house every night at 7:00pm sharp to visit his mother for 1 hour was clearly imprinted in the grassy slope. The little bridge over the stream and the path are now gone. But both homes that are part of my childhood memories are still there. We were taught as children to be proud of our heritage and name. They gave me roots, Great Grandma (GG) and Great Grandpa (Jack). Engaged 9/16/07 and married 4/03/09. The dates inscribed inside the simple wedding band that I now wear on my right hand.

I remember so well being told to be proud of our family name and where we came from. Rely on our strength from inside. Stand tall with dignity and always remember who our ancestors were that came before us. Honor them in how we conducted ourselves.

My Grandma Wilma putting her finger against my heart when I was eight and stating very emphatically that what is inside counts. It did not matter what we had or what church we went to. What was important was the love inside and that we knew God lived there.

Planted Roots

My roots are planted in the past
Growing strong and true so they may last
My strength is centered in my roots
Having grown from generations ago
Roots spread far and deep
To hold my trunk tall and straight
With branches strengthened by my core
Not a bush but a tree
That Lives and grows with splendid dignity

Speak Through Me

Speak through me my angels of light
Keep me safe in your morning light
Hold me close when darkness falls
Cradle me lest I stumble and fall
May your word fill the page
Where I've laid my pen gently in wait

My Grandma Wilma was and is also still an influence in my day to day life. She always told me to believe in myself. What was inside was what was important. She was an amazing lady whom imprinted herself on my siblings and myself. We adored her…. This poem is about not just my grandmother, but also my mother, her mother and her mother before her…. I would sit on grandma's lap and trace the veins in her hands and feel her essence and energy as a child. So, for all my father's mothers and mothers' mothers many generations back this is the poem that flowed onto my page.

Her Hands

Her hands held me when I was a just babe
Her hands washed me as I grew each day
Her hands kept me sheltered daily from all harm
Her hands I rushed to when I needed warmth
Her hands guided me from the day I was born
Her hands were my guidance even when she was worn
Her hands I remember each day
When I look down at my hands and see the simple way
The simple way I've guided my own and loved them each day
My hands are rough and worn from my daily share
My hands are stiff and swollen from the constant wear
My hand is here to hold them when they need my care
My hands are filled with healing for those who ask of me
My hands are reminders of when I was a babe
When her hands held me closely and taught me to not be afraid
I look down now at my hands and realize it is true
My hands are my mother's hands and her mother's too.......

Dedicated to my Grandma Wilma. My Angel

When my grandmother passed, she was 95. I was in Eastern Washington, my daddy called me to let me know. I went to my hotel room. She'd had a stroke 3 years' prior that took her short-term memory. Her left side was completely paralyzed and she could not communicate clearly. She spoke with a very pronounced slur. She was now helpless as a baby and she hated it. I would go visit her and tell her who I was. She knew my voice and her clear blue eyes would light up and twinkle. Then slowly her beautiful smile would light up her face.

I thought about her all that evening. About her warmth, her smile, how her eyes sparkled when she laughed. And the smell of her Estee Lauder perfume she always wore. How this amazing woman made her three little grandkids who felt lost after our parents divorced, did her best to keep our family connection alive. The love she had for her family. How she conducted herself in public. She owned a little dress shop. She never left the house unless she was perfectly coiffed. "No one would see her not looking her best". Making her grandkids get their own switch off the willow tree when we miss-behaved. She'd play in the yard with us, doing cart wheels when required. Or she would sit with grandpa on the covered patio watching, listening to the birds. Enjoying the humming birds visit the begonia and fuchsia baskets that grandpa planted. Not to mention the feeders that were hung everywhere. They had their own little bird watching area in their yard that the Audubon Society would have envied. That was grandma, a business woman who at heart just simply loved life uncomplicated.

I said my prayers that night, told her I loved her and thanked her for all the wonderful memories. The next morning, I got up still thinking about her, her humor, her joy in life. I was talking out loud to her, got in the shower still talking to her. Next thing I know the shower that was at a gentle flow is on full bore blast mode going hot and cold. Then it stopped. Scared me to death and then I just said "Okay Grandma, got it, you are still here" And she has been since.

I was also influenced by my mother's mother, Edythe. She grew up in North Dakota by her mother Jesse who divorced her husband when Edythe was just a girl. Grandma did not have it easy. She married my grandfather when she was just 15. They conceived 12 children. 11 lived to adulthood. In her bare feet, she stretched to 4'8" s. She had a sweet bawdy sense of humor. When asked why she had all those kids. Her response was simple. "When grandpa hung his pants on the bedpost. I knew there was another baby on the way". Then she would shrug her shoulders and laugh with joy. They were poor yet her home and all the kids were neat and clean. She quoted many times "We may not have had much, but soap is cheap." She had a weekly work schedule that for years never changed. Monday, she made bread and donuts. That was the day to visit grandma! Or Thursdays when she made cookies. The kitchen counters were lined with cookie jars. For her cookie monsters as she called us. Her home had grandkids daily running through it. Tuesday was wash day. If you were lucky she would let you ride the washer around the kitchen while it danced during the spin cycle. She'd lift you on it and tell you to keep it in place. She bought gifts all year long for Christmas so each of her grandkids had a gift from her and grandpa. One year she crocheted afghan blankets for each of us, another we received bath towels and wash clothes with our initials embroidered on them.

I was blessed with huge family gatherings at all the Holidays. There were 47 grandchildren. There has been debate about it with my cousins. 39 is the count they have. But I clearly remember my grandmother saying to me there were 47 total. And Grandma kept track of us all! So, I called my Mom and asked her to help me. I listed each Aunt and Uncle's name, then below each grandchild's name including step grandchildren. My grandma did not exclude because a child was not born into her family, she accepted you as a grandchild and called you that. And the list grew. But we were not at 47, still 8 short. The next question was "How many Mom passed away like my little baby brother, or who were not part of our family for whatever reason? There were 4 that were adopted out when two of my aunts had babies out of wedlock, 1 from an Uncle who had an affair, and 3 babies like my little brother who did not survive infancy. 47 total. This poem is in dedication to Mary Edythe. She made our childhood perfect.

Forty-Seven Angels

Forty-Seven Angels sent from above
To feel her love and care
In her arms, we found safety there
And as we grew so did she
Her heart and arms stretched to capacity
And as she aged she never wept
But kept us in her safety net
Then one day heaven called
While her forty-seven angels wept
As she passed we gave her to our God in need
Her forty-seven Angels earthen bound
Still feel her loving arms and care
As she is now our Angel there
That God has sent to give us love
And as we leave our Earthly place
She'll welcome us at heaven's gate

Dedicated to my Grandma, my Angel: Edythe

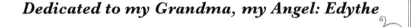

12

The rest of this book is for those who have been through any type of violence in their lives. I hope my poetry brings understanding and healing if even in a small way. We do not heal overnight and some of our wounds never heal. But we can learn from our pasts. And we can all open ourselves up to our Angels and ask for their guidance. God gave us the ability to love each other and help each other be better souls. He sent to each of us Angels. It is up to us to listen, feel them and know they are there.

This poem represents my past and my future. My past is filled with pain and sorrow not just for myself but also my husband. We had Love Laughter and Joy in our lives for the 26 total years we were together. Yet the pain and sorrow is what defined our life together. We both had tumultuous childhoods. For myself I was determined not to let my childhood define and control my future. I cannot speak for my husband. But what I do know is that he never forgave himself or his family for what happened to him as a child. That pain festered into the anger that he directed towards me.

Box of Sorrow

In my mind is a shelf of boxes
Each clearly labeled
Love, Joy, Laughter, Pain and Sorrow
I reach for Sorrow once again
And hold it in my hands
As I untie the ribbon and lift the lid
I let undeniable, mind numbing,
Heart wrenching Sorrow unfold
Relive the memories I have endured
Feel the tears wet my face as they fall
Quietly put the Sorrow away to relive another day
Tie the ribbon to hold my feelings in
And remember why I live facing forward in each day

One of the first signs of my husband's anger was him throwing stuff, jumping up and down in the middle of a room, fists clenched and literally foaming at the mouth while screaming through clenched teeth. I was scared but determined to help make him feel better. Not understanding that there was nothing I could do to help him. I took on the role of appeasing him. Do not anger him, always telling him I was sorry that I upset him. I became the focus of his anger.

Over the years I repaired stairway hand rails that he`ripped off walls. Holes in walls where his fists hit. Holes from door handles when he threw open doors and the door knob went into the walls. The entire door frames from him slamming doors so hard that it cracked the frame. A kitchen counter that spider cracked after he'd slammed his fist on it. Kitchen and bathroom cabinet doors and drawers that were ripped from the hinges. Drawer frames cracked from being slammed or my body being slammed against it. These things were my fault as I was told time and time again. If I had not angered him, He would not have broken our things and acted the way he did.

He actually broke the driver's seat of our Ford Bronco while driving down the freeway. He asked me for directions and I was reading the road map. In the late 80's/early 90's there was not GPS. You had road maps. He is getting upset with me, which always made me terrified and not able to articulate the answer fast. Next thing I know he is slamming his fists into his head, screaming at me that I am a fucking bitch and stupid. I am crying at him "Please! put your hands on the wheel, I am sorry, I am sorry, you are going to kill us!" He then puts his clenched fists around the steering wheel and starts slamming his body backwards into the driver's seat. We heard the seat frame crack! That got his attention, he looks at me and says, "You fucking bitch, you made me break the seat." He was mad at me every time he drove the Bronco after that. All I knew was that I needed to appease him so that it did not happen again. And I was so thankful that our son was not with us. This was the first temper fit that truly scared me. But I was determined to make my marriage work. And now I had a little baby boy to think of too.

Pieces of Me

Pieces of me were shattered to bits
When he would kick, hit and spit
Pieces of me that made me whole
Strewn about and trampled down
Piece by piece my soul was strewn
Piece by piece my home was ruined
Piece by piece my mind was shattered
Piece by piece my heart was tattered
Little by little I am building up
Picking up pieces that were lost
Little pieces that have been hiding
Little pieces I'd forgotten about
Pieces of my soul I've found
Pieces of my heart rebound
Pieces of my mind open up
I pick them up and dust them off
And like a puzzle put them in
They do not all fit like they should
Some still missing, some not right
It may take years to build myself
Piece by piece it was taken apart
Piece by piece I build again......

My daughter was 11 months old when he started to hit me. We had gone to a baseball game at local stadium on a week day, just the two of us. We decided to go out to dinner too. I called the sitter, made the arrangements, and picked up the kids from daycare. We got dressed up. I actually remember in detail what we wore and ate for dinner. The memories of this night tragically imprinted forever in my mind. I had on a yellow linen summer dress. He wore his linen slacks, paired with a white t-shirt and navy blue linen blazer. We went to a popular restaurant that overlooks the bay. To get there you travel up a steep twisting two lane road to the top of the hill. We ordered scallops for me and he had Cioppino, seafood stew. Over dinner we had drinks and he was getting upset about the lack of service. This was normal behavior for him when we went out. Then he started to direct his anger towards me. I am trying to keep him calm in public, defuse his anger towards our server. At some point, he decided that I was not listening properly to him. Even though I could repeat our conversation back to him. I emphatically told him that I would drive home. He'd had too much to drink, he agreed for once.

We got in the car and I had just started down the hill. Suddenly I feel his fist slam into the right side of my head. I am now trying to steer the car down this hill with a steep embankment on the right. Using my right arm to shield myself from the blows against my head and right upper body. He is literally punching me as I drive. I am crying out for him to stop. At the bottom of the hill there is a stop sign. He finally stopped hitting me, but the language he is spewing at me is horrific. I kept asking what did I do. He replies, you did not listen to me properly. Then he jumped out of the car. I am in shock and speed away. All I knew in that moment is I must get my babies.

I drove home. I must have looked a sight to our sitter. I had put a sweater on over my shoulders to hide my bruises. My right side of my head I could feel lumps forming from his fists. I did not want her to see them nor did I want to see them or my babies to see them. I put the kids in the car, made some excuse as to why he was not with me. Took the sitter to her home and drove back towards the restaurant trying to find my husband. With my five-year-old son and little baby, girl in the back seat.

Knowing I need to find him because all hell would break loose if I did not. And asking myself what do I do now? How do I take care of my babies on my salary, how do we survive? How do I fix this and make it better? How did I keep my babies from growing up without their daddy like I did?

Hit me now came to me one day while driving. I was driving between stores in my district. Remembering and thinking about what my ex-husband would call me. And acknowledging to myself that I would be thankful after he hit me. Because then I would not have to hear all the awful things he said to me for a while. And I did not have to feel the fear of knowing he was going to hit me again.

Hit me now

Go ahead, Do your deed
Get it over, make it stop
The words you spew crush my thoughts
Hit me now I silently plead
Words of hate you call your mate
Words so cruel, they topple my world
Fucking cunt, bitch and whore
Until I cannot take it anymore
Hit me now, Get it over
For when you hit, I find solace
That your words of hate will abate

I learned over the years of what is known as the honeymoon stage of DV. The abuser tells the victim that it will never happen again and they shower the victim with gifts and love. And I so wanted to believe him. Did my husband love me? Yes, he did. Did he intentionally try to hurt me? No I don't think so. But he was like a light switch. One-minute fine, the next CLICK!!! This person of anger took over. And when he hit, all the name calling, belittling would stop when he was done. And I had my husband, my best friend and love back. Until the switch went on again.

The switch would go off and on over the next eleven years. I was isolated more and more from my family. We went to see his family for most holidays. Going to see my family meant that the switch would go on the day prior or the night prior. If the switch did not get switched, then it was listening to how horrible my family was and how much he hated them as he belittled them to myself and our children. To argue meant taking the chance of the switch being switched on. So, learning to just listen and even agree meant safety to myself and my children being protected from them hearing him belittle and abuse me. I was very good at seeing the switch and telling my babies to go their rooms.

I made the final choice to leave after he had attacked me on a Saturday or Sunday morning. The kids were not home. I'd taken a bath and was in our bedroom getting dressed. Next thing I know the bedroom door is slammed open, he is standing over me where I was sitting on the bed naked. He is screaming and foaming at the mouth "Your stupid bitch! God, I hate you! You fucking cunt!" He grabs me by the neck and straddles me while choking me as I am laying under him across our bed. He kept screaming at me and shaking me with his hands around my throat and I am choking, trying to breathe. Then just as soon as he had started, he quits, jumps up and slams back out of our bedroom. I remember laying there naked sobbing, realizing he could have killed me and what happens next time? Do I stay? Do I go? Who do I turn to? My family did not know; I rarely saw them anymore. What about my kids? My son and My daughter needed both parents, didn't they?

The following poems do not need explanations. They are about my mindset, gathering my inner strength. Hardening my heart with the knowledge that the only way for me to survive was to take a leap of faith and leave. Knowing that I may lose my children but I had to try for them and for myself. And failure was not an option for me.

One Shares

How does one Share
The feeling of intense despair
Despairs that leaves you feeling hollow
Despair that makes the heavens weep
From a hurt that drives so deep
Despair from a love gone cold
Despair of heart, mind and soul
Despair from words too hateful to hear
Despair caused by cuts and bruises
Delivered by the hands of one who
Promised to love, honor, and cherish
One looks within and gathers strength
One asks for guidance from above
One hardens their heart, mind and soul
One takes the steps into the unknown
Knowing it is better than the despair felt there
One makes the decision to live with love
and nothing less, even if it means loneliness.

Done!

I'll try harder were my words
When he would rant, hit and hurt
I'm sorry, sorry was my plea
When he would kick and spit on me
It's all your fault he would yell
You've made me angry and act this way
It's all your fault he would scream
All your fault you've angered me
All my fault was to love
All my fault to keep the hope
All my fault to never bend
All my fault I kept within
Then one day I said no more
I'm done with you keeping score
I'm done with pleading
Done with trying
Sick of being scared to speak
Sick of being your beating board
It's not my fault, it is yours
For not keeping our love
from crumbling down
It is your fault I laid at your feet
So I would never have to spend
Another day on my knees
Praying with tears, God help me please.

Thankful is for me the poem that for me is hauntingly real every time I read it. I do not know how to express the shame one has after being hit, slammed into walls and choked. There are no words to describe this shame. But I hope this one poem explains that despair felt. And how I had to harden my heart against my husband. I still have people ask me why I left my children with him. I really did not have a choice. I had to leave, so I could save them.

Thankful

She sits is in wonder in the night
Thankful that she has survived
Tears of shame across her face
That by morning there be will no trace
No trace of the anger she has endured
And as dawn breaks her bruises ache
But not a sound will she make
She'll keep them hidden until they heal
And make her heart a brick of steel
Cool grey cold is how it feels
All her senses have shut down
Even when her tears cascade down
There is no laughter in her eyes
Only the bleakness that his fists have solidified
She knows her days are numbered now
Limited days until she escapes
It is the only choice for her to make
She leaves her family with a prayer
A prayer to keep them safe from his anger there

There Is...

There is a smile upon her face
That hides the pain of love erased
There is a tear upon her cheek
That defines the world she leaves
There is a depth within her eyes
That defies the tragedy in her mind
There is a bruise upon her lips
That tells the world of a life amiss
There is a life that she knew
That she leaves behind to start anew

Strength of a Thousand Men

Enough already! I said to him
I've endured your hurt one last time
For I've the Strength of a thousand men
For I was given just one heart
A heart to love with
A heart to share
A heart meant to be handled with care
But, you have bruised it
Abused it, stomped it down
Taken it for granted until I was on the hard cold ground
Begging you to stop the hurt
That you spewed and threw around
My heart is tattered
The life we had all in shreds
Yet my strength was there
And I relied instead
On my strength within of a thousand men...

The following poems describe for me how isolating, controlled, I felt and I now know I am not the only one to have felt this way. But as I prayed for help and started to connect with my heavenly father and my Angels, I knew I was no longer alone.

Alone in the Crowd

Alone in the crowd
Standing tall
She's felt alone since
She was small
She hides her hurt
Behind her pride
And never shows
The longing inside
On her face
Is a mask
To hide the feelings
She conceals
One look in her eyes
Will reveal
Her wish to belong
She stands tall
Alone in the crowd
Since she was small

Darkness in Me

In my soul is a place I know
A place of darkness where sorrow grows
A place of hurt and despair
A place of this earth that belongs nowhere
I block this place from my mind
Ask my angels of divine
To heal this place in my soul
That only God in heaven knows
God hears my pleas of helplessness
When the darkness in me insists
Insists to let it take me down
Down in the darkness for me to drown
My angels God sent to me
Guard my soul and destiny
And lifts me up with Heavens care
This care sent down from above
To heal my soul with Angelic love

There Is...

There is a smile upon her face
That hides the pain of love erased
There is a tear upon her cheek
That defines the world she leaves
There is a depth within her eyes
That defies the tragedy in her mind
There is a bruise upon her lips
That tells the world of a life amiss
There is a life that she knew
That she leaves behind to start anew

Lone Tear

A lone tear in her eye
Trace of the past gone by
Her laughter hides the sorrow known
Her smile speaks of yet to come
She sees a future shown to her
Through her angelic gift bestowed.

In Reply

I bowed my head again today
And prayed once more my soul to take
And in reply I heard
Too soon, for you've much work to do...

This is poem based upon the dream I had prior to meeting my husband for the first time. I had this dream when I was 16. I met him a year later when I was 17. But the groom in the dream looked like the young man in my dream. When I met him the first time it was like "Oh! There you are." The dream of my wedding day. After I met him I prayed that we would be blessed and I asked God to help me help him. I can say that God does answer prayers.

I Dreamed a Dream

I dreamed a dream
All dressed in white
With my husband by my side
I prayed to god that this be true
To give me strength to see us through
I loved him through all the years
Yet my heart broke from all the tears
My soul was strong and stayed in tact
God's love made clear as I asked
His guidance in each day and
For my Angels help along the way.

The following poem came to me as I thought of my children. How their life was impacted by DV. I still remember with clarity telling my children to go to their rooms. Each time I could tell that my husband, their father was going to snap. I did not want them to see, witness, my humiliation. But they could still hear and they knew. Afterwards I would go check on them. My daughter would be in her room with her ear phones on listening to music, humming to it while on her bed. She acted like nothing was wrong, all defense mechanisms in place. My son would be in the corner of his room, huddled against the wall with his lamb and lambie blanket pressed to his face. Crying with such sorrow. No child should be so stoic or so hurt that they cannot comprehend that someone they love could hurt them to this extent.

Weep as we Sleep

Children Weep
As we sleep
Tears fill their eyes
Pain enfolds
From wounds
We are told
Inflicted by
Anger unjustified
Pain fills their souls
Their stories untold
Silenced by needs
To just please
The ones they love
Not understanding
The cruelty directed
Their innocence affected
Our children weep
As we sleep

This poem is from my experience in childhood. There was a two-year period where my step grandfather molested me. This poem is important because what happened did impact how I viewed the world. And this is when I started to not listen to my angels. It was the end of my innocence of being a child. I was 8 years old, innocent and wanting to please my new family members.

Fairies Prayer

Fairies gather all around
The little figure on the ground
They offer words of love to her
Word of wisdom to heal her hurt
A hurt so deep it makes her weep
Her soul and heart, bitter and bleak
That another could make her feel this unclean
Unclean and uninvited was his touch
But a touch he had to have
This very very selfish man
How can this child understand?
The unclean mind of this man
She knows she cannot stay
in the safety of her forest place
As she listens to those around
They send her out and on her way
She always knows when they are there
For they hear her fairies' prayers

For my Father-in-Law. May he heal his son now he's an Angel. My Ex's story is not mine to tell. It is his. What I can say, other then what happened in his childhood made him the man I married. And he needed to forgive his family to learn to love and be the caring loving man I knew he could be. I've learned that I cannot heal someone with my love. Only they can heal themselves. He has his demons that caused the switch and because of my own childhood trauma, it helped the switch go on. I am not saying I am anyway to blame for the DV. I am not. Yet the dysfunction of my childhood made me accept the blame he placed on me. He knew I would do just about anything to keep my marriage and our little family intact.

Heal your Son

How do you tell your Son, Dad?
How do you tell your Son?
That you are bitter and empty for the things you've done

How do you tell your Son, Dad?
How do you tell your Son?
That all you ever wanted was for him to feel your love.

How do you heal your Son Dad?
How do you heal your Son?
The one thing that was needed to mend his open wounds.

How do you love your Son Dad?
How do you love your Son?
When you are passed and cannot reach beyond your grave.

How do you tell you tell your Dad, Son?
How do you tell your Dad?
That what he did has wedged a wall around his heart and yours.

How do you forgive your Dad, Son?
How do you forgive your Dad?
When all you can do is feel the empty bitter hate.

How do you love your Dad, Son?
How do you love your Dad?
When all that is left, is a headstone on his grave.

Dedicated to Debbie.
A woman I never knew on this earth
She'd suffered too much pain through
DV. But I know of this pain
And what it does to the human mind and soul.
And I also know she is another Angel by my side.

Her Despair beyond Repair

Pulled down in the depths one day
The only way she knew to make her pain go away
A pain caused by the love of past
A pain that was not meant to last
Her weakened spirit was all she had left
Her heart and soul too bruised to heal
Thinking death was her only hope to never feel
Never feel the loss of her being
Never feel her despair beyond repair
Trampled down by years of heartache
Day after day of hopelessness
Her soul too broken to ever heal
She made a choice to never ever feel
Never realizing the hurt left behind
When she decided to take her life
So beautiful Angel use your wings
To guide and heal your family

I learned of Debbie through a man I dated for close to a year. And during this year I started to hear my angels through dreams and yes sometimes just as they spoke to me as they had when I was a child. I knew they were back and I was starting to hear them again. I had opened my mind back up through prayers and just quiet time. I had not started to write my poems yet. But it was the beginning. He had once stated to me that he wanted someone who wrote poems and put them in his lunch or left them around the house. I was like, I don't believe in that mushy stuff. I kind of scoffed at him about it.

I had been married 24 years with DV. Then, with another man for 4 years who lived off my good heart and tried to control me through my love of my children. And to top it off dated another man for 9 months, that dated another behind my back. He met her at a wedding that I could not go to, due to my job in retail and it being the "back to school season". I was working all Saturdays that August. The day of the wedding I was driving back home through Eastern Washington. Like many years before I knew. I just knew, I heard in my head "He has found another." Two weeks later he took me to dinner, would not look at me in the face, kept looking over my shoulder out the window. He told me when he dropped me off at home. I did not date for 7 months. Then I thought well it is time to get out and live again.

I met Walter. During the time, I dated Walter my Angels started to communicate very clearly. Although I did not understand what they were telling me. Walter had told me about Debbie, she was his fiancé and had committed suicide. She'd had her demons from her marriage filled with DV. She walked into a lake and drowned herself. I had told Walter about my marriage and I was the first woman he had dated a year after her death. During the first 3 months that we dated, I had a dream.

"Walter was driving this flatbed truck and I was tied down on the back of it. He was driving fast through the woods then the truck slows and goes through this little town. There is a bend in the middle of it. This tall man with dark hair and black clothes comes running out of a saloon in this town. He runs after the truck but cannot reach me. Then truck drives around a bend into the woods and up the hills into the mountains. Walter pulls over and drops me off in the dark woods alongside the road.

I wander around in the woods then he comes back and picks me up and we go to the end of the road where we stand and look over a bay."

A month later Walter is telling me he does not know if he wants to be with me. He is confused and does not know what he feels. I was devastated, but was determined not to cry over spilt milk and just date others. I met a great man who was very tall, dark haired and dressed in dark clothes. He did not drink; he was a recovering alcoholic. Angels were talking! After 4 weeks Walter calls me, brings me a bouquet from his garden of lavender and daylilies. Walter and I went on vacation in the San Juan islands and we did hike to the top of a Mountain and gazed out over the Puget Sound. I was ecstatic. I had told the man I had just started to date that Walter was back. But my Angels still had more messages for me. A few weeks later I had another dream

"I entered this stone house from the garage below into the dark where I had seen Walter go in. I cannot find him. I enter a hot-tub in the room. It turns into a deep dark well and I am drowning in the murky leaf filled water, I get to the top of the water and Walter walks by. I am naked and shaken, I call to him he just walks down the dark stairs next to me. I follow him outside I cannot find him. I run back into the stone house up the dark stairs. I look out large glass window and there below on the side walk is Walter walking away with a brunette woman beside him holding his hand. I am standing naked shivering and completely alone."

Three months later Walter has told me he does not know what he feels and just needs to be alone. My Angels were showing me messages that they knew I needed. I was alone again.

I started to write. The poems just started to flow after this. I know the dream message was from Debbie through the drowning in my dream. And Walter did not tell me there was someone else. I had been shown.

I lost my grandma during the 9 months Walter and I dated. My daddy gave me my great grandmothers wedding ring during this period and I have not taken it off since I received it. I just know GG sends me the poems and messages. I tapped into my angels now more than ever. I needed their messages, their guidance, their love and their strength.

Path of Reality

Bitter, confused, broken, hollow
Love has left and I swallow
The reality of life lessons burn
Lessons learned through many turns
Until my heart never strays
From this lonely path I take
A path of darkness where I cry

Loneliness seeps from my eyes
As I realize it is only I to prop me up
Only I to travel alone
Only I to watch the stars
Up in the darkened sky
God has not left me here
He's only said you have
To travel alone on this path
A path that leads to your destiny

Tears

How many times have I cried?
Felt the tears fall from my eyes
Tears releases to cleanse my soul
Tears to heal as I let go
Tears of sorrow for the last time
Tears of pain
Tears of hope that went away
Oh, how many times have I cried?
Felt the tears fall from my eyes
Tears of love
Tears of joy
Tears of laughter through the years
Oh, how many times have I cried?
Felt the tears fall from my eyes
Tears released to cleanse my soul
Tears to heal as I let go…..

Hidden Sadness

A place within my soul
A place where sadness grows
A place a lost love hides
A place only I can set aside
As I face each day
I set this hidden place away
Someday this place will be forgotten
As my soul starts to love again….

Well of Sorrow

A well of sorrow fills my soul.
Only my faith has kept me whole
Faith of lesson God's sent to me
Have given me strength and dignity
Life lessons learned, Life lessons taught
His wealth of love bestowed to me as I pray
From the well within my soul
Sorrow subsides and love still grows

Letting Go

Release the sorrow in your soul
There is no shame in doing so
Joy abounds in letting go
No good comes from hanging on
Forgive yourself and move on
Forgive those who have hurt you too
This will help you start living anew
Send them love from your heart
And realize they are who they are
Nothing you can do will help
They have to try and help themselves
Only you can change your life
The same for them if they try
Look at your life with new eyes
And your blessings are multiplied
But hanging on to the past
Will only lead you down that path.
Release the sorrow in your soul
Joy abounds in letting go

Wounded Souls Forgive

Does one forgive
the anger shown
Does one forget
the anger known
One looks inside
and draws a breath
To see the answers there
We're given time
to heal our wounds
From the wounded soul
That delivered blows
Who never knew
to forgive is to forget
Wounded souls forgive
For in forgiveness
Love is found and
Your soul will rebound

Safe in Angels Wings for me is beautiful. I thank God each night as I pray for my family of Angels. I call each of them by name and send them my love. I always start with "I love you daddy" and just keep going until I am done. There are times I sit on my couch and I feel a very light touch in my hair. Like it is being played with. I know daddy is there.

Safe in Angels Wings

I sleep at night wrapped in light
Safe in Angels Wings
They hold me close,
Give me hope,
And gently comfort me
As I dream they show me a place
Lit with luminous skies
Where children play without a care
Safe in the love they share
Where hurt is unknown
And healing is shown
To all who enter there
While asleep my soul is at peace
When I awake, their wings unfurl
As I uncurl to start another day
With their promise of protection
I bestow them my affections
Safe in Angels wings

This poem came from an experience just after Walter left. I was so devastated, and felt so alone. I cried myself to sleep for weeks. The last 6 years has not been easy and I had learned so many lessons. It must have been about 3:00AM in the morning, I was waking up like I do most nights at about 3:00 in the wee hours. I realize my grandpa is sitting on the edge of the bed. He is in his light slacks, a brown sweater like he always wore and his fedora on his head. He is facing away from me. But next to him is my black cat Murphy lying next to him facing the same way as grandpa with his head up being petted. Then I hear quite clearly "Oops! Gotta Go" Then grandpa is gone. But the feeling of comfort knowing that he was watching over me in my time of sorrow and need was uplifting. This is when I accepted I was not alone, my family was with me.

My Path

My path is clear
When he is near
My Path is wide
With his Angels by my side
When it Narrows
And is cast shadows
I've allowed my doubts
To cloud my mind
And my fears to darken my steps
But when I stop and take a breath
Enfold his Angels hands in mine
The shadows lift and fear disappear
To my grateful delight
My Path is lit in pure light
Once again I am on my way
Living each moment
Within each day

This poem came from a dream where I was on a path that had many dark places on it. But I just kept focused on staying in the light. And there were 3 others with me on this path. Pointing the out the direction I needed to go.

Listen Quietly

Listen quietly in the night
You will hear to your delight
Angelic voices all around
Voices sent with messages bold
Voices sent with messages to be told
Sent to lift your spirit each day
Sent to heal your heart and soul
Words of love will come to you
Words of joy and happiness
All you need is your faith
An open heart to receive God's grace
Listen quietly in the night
And hear Angels sing with delight.

A Place

In her mind is a place
A place she goes to escape
Where Angels speak from above
And feel the healing of God's love
A place she goes to gather strength
To prepare her for another day

Family of Angels

My family of angels grows and grows
Each step I take another is shown
Shown in the sky, cloudy or blue
Shown in the grasses that rustle anew
They meet me with laughter and delight
They whisper their knowledge in the darkness of night
They speak to my heart, and they touch my soul
And help my mind to acknowledge their souls
Listen softly and you will hear
Your family of Angels is always near

Answered Prayers

God answers prayers everyday
Some prayers are only answered
In challenges we have been shown
For many years my world was black
As I prayed and prayed
Believing that my father above
Had left me during my darkest days
And as my world turn from black to grey
I continued to pray and pray
Believing that there would be better days
And slowly the grey turned to white
And my heart washed in heavenly light
Through it all he was there
Sending angels to shelter me
With his grace and care

Angels Travel came to me after a dream I had about my territory in Eastern Washington. I had 5 stores close together in one city. One manager was what I call a swizzle stick and another manager that was on drugs. My Group leader was protecting them.

"*I could see the City blowing up. I was trying to get to my one manager that I knew I needed to keep. She was my ally in the whole mess. I had to get to her, but I know I have to go around all the obstacles and I need to get above the floods and fires. I am on this dirt path leading out of the City. I must climb up this dirt cliff with a large pig in my way. I look back and there are three figures dressed in long robes, their heads are covered in hoods with long staffs in their hands. Garments from biblical times is what I saw. They see me looking back and very quickly they point with their staffs the direction beyond the pig I need to take. I turn and keep going in that direction, climb over the pig and get to the top of the cliff. Where I can see the damage in the valley below*"

Angels travel with me

My Angels travel with me
Of this I have no doubt
My Angels safely guide me
On each path I go down
My angels gently catch me
When I stumble all about
My angels quickly lift me up
When I am turned around
And place me back on my path
And point me in the way
That God wants me to take
They whisper softly to my heart
Not to be afraid.
My Angels have been with me
Since I was but a tot
My angels never judged me
When I was grown and lost
My Angels listened closely
And heard my every prayer
When I thought I was all alone
And my heart was in despair
My Angels will be with me
Each and every step
My Angels will travel with me
Of this I have no doubt

I termed the manager that was on drugs 3 weeks later, the swizzle stick walked, when I fired the first manager. My group leader quit and I kept the manager that I was trying to get to. Angels were guiding me and showing me the way. I was mystified by the three men in my dream. I kept thinking about them, this dream and trying to understand their significance. A few days later I am pulling over on the side of the freeway to write a poem about Miriam, Abram and Saul. Spirit Guides one and all. A few months later I am in bed just waking up and I hear in my left ear. "Miriam" in this electronic sounding voice. More confirmation that God had sent his Angels to help me.

Angels Around

There are Angels all around
Listen quietly
They can be found
Singing softly of God's word
Gently call and you will be heard
Look deep inside you will find
Your soft request has been blessed

Angelic Chorus

My Angels abound
In life all around
They speak sweetly to me
Of life's harmony
They show me I'm blessed
In love and forgiveness
Softly they sing
In my hour of need
And lift my heart
Out of the dark
Into god's holy light
Pure Angelic voices
Sing in a chorus of white.

This poem came from another dream I had.

"I am wandering on this path and come to my home. It is in the middle of the forest. I go through the little gate in the middle of the stone fence, I follow the granite path to the door of the cabin. The yard is just bare stumps. I go inside and there is a huge stone fireplace that takes up one wall. I hear noise coming from behind the stones. A scratching, I start to take the stones down one by one. Until I uncover a huge bear sleeping. He wakes and I start to yell at him to leave. I am now yelling at this bear "Walter get out of my house leave me be. Stay away from me, Go!"

Well, Walter did come back into my life 6 months later. We had three days together and then he told me he had a girlfriend. I told him never to contact me again and to stay away from me. I have not heard from him since. What I find incredible every time I have one of "MY DREAMS" is that they happen prior to my life experiences. Angels talking to me in my dreams.

Release

Today it's time to say goodbye
To one who meant so much
For my love was not enough
To heal your wounded soul
You were given a choice
To take my hand
And feel the love unfold
Instead you chose to stay in place
Inside the world you mold
A world of toil and conflict
Of which you hold so close
For it was easier for you to stay
Then reach out and take my hand
Feel the breeze of life's gifts
To open with surprise
And face the joy at hand

Essence of Souls

How many fractures
Can a heart take?
A heart that heals
And then again breaks
It is the essence of
Souls to find
One to love for all time

Blessings sent from above

Blessings sent from above
Showered down and feel his love
Open up to this world
And feel the blessing sent unfurl

Choose your life everyday
Choose to live in a darkened haze
Or choose to open up and feel
Feel a love that helps you heal

Feel the rhythms in this world
Feel the lives that you touch
God's blessed each of us
And showered us in everlasting love.

Clarity

When you listen
Close at hand
You will hear the words
Of many voices
Voices from your past
Will give you love and clarity
Clarity of your past
Clarity of love too last
Wisdom comes in many forms
Forms of love evermore
Listen to the words they speak
Words of love and family...

Bond of Love

Only Faith will see us through
Faith in myself and faith in you
Faith sent down from above
To help us heal and seal our love
Faith in this bond that hold us tight
Faith in our love surrounded in pure light
A love of strength formed by our bond
Never severed for which I wait….

A dream I had prompted this poem.

"I was holding on to the hands of a little girl with short brown hair that framed her chubby face. Dressed in a printed flannel nightgown. Below her was nothing but darkness. I knew if I let go she would swirl into the darkness."

The emotional pain of the thought of letting go was so real and extreme I woke up silently crying with my heart pounding. I always felt it was God and my Angels telling me to hold on tight to my inner strength and faith. That the little girl was still inside, I just needed to nourish her and hold on.

Holding

Holding on to my inner Child
Holding on to her grace and charm
Holding on to the little girl
That knows how to dance in this world
Holding her with arms wide open
As she laughs twists and twirls
Holding on to her innocence
And knowing that she's been blessed
Holding on to my inner child
As she wishes upon the stars
Holding on to my inner child as she
Gazes up to the Twinkling Heavens
Bathed in the pale moon light
Holding on to my inner child
She has the strength to see life through.

Bear with me Angels

Bear with me angels
For I am only human
My soul was sent to earth
Through my choice I was given
My heavenly father granted me
Another lesson in this realm
To heal another in this life
And make his presence felt
Please bear with him Angels
For he is only human
And his earthly fears
Have taken o'er his soul
Please pray with me angels
And send my love to him
To heal his heart, touch his soul
That he may love again,
Please pray for us Angels
For we are only human
Help us find our hearts
To love and heal our souls
In this earthly realm
Please pray with us angels
And hold our earthly forms
So we may never cry again.

Path of Faith

Have faith in the path you're on
For God's Angels guide you on
Be free to explore each turn and road
For his Angels will lighten your path
And when darkness shadows your soul
God's light and love will lighten your load
Faith is all you need each day
And if you've strayed upon your way
Let his loving Angels guide you back

Army of Angels

My army of angels
Visit me each night
As I sleep
They hold me close,
Comfort me
Soothe my soul
Bring me peace
As I awake
Face the day
They kneel with me
As I pray
Heavenly Father up above
Send my love to those in need
And give me strength
To start my day

Words of Angels

Listen quietly to your heart
Hear the words your angels impart
Words of wisdom, Words of love
To help you live within each day
Listen closely to what they say
Joy will be found as you pray
Listen closely to the wind and air
Soft laughter will tell you when they are near
Feel the warmth of their love
When your soul is wrapped in soft white wings
Feel your heart soar to the sky
Where angels gather with you for all time

Awakened

I've been awakened within my soul
Heaven's light within me flows
Surrounded by the one's I love
My life is touched from above
I feel the cry from those in need
They see my light and come to me
I speak to them of divine love
And direct them to his healing light
My loved one's take them by the hand
And guide them to his promise land
And as they pass through Heaven's gate
They find peace where their loved ones wait.

Reach...

Reach in your heart
Receive God's grace
For in a moment
Your prayers take place
He listens diligently to
Your pleas in prayer
And answers your request
When it is made clear
So lift your heart
Clear your mind
For God answers prayers
When you lay your soul bare.

Dedicated to Daddy, John Allen

Daddy passed away 3 years ago. He had a heart attack at his cabin he and my stepmom had built. It was his favorite place to be.

He was now visiting me and guiding in his own way.

Alone Today

I walk this path alone today
Understanding you've gone way
For on this path I must travel alone
To heal and find myself again
And as I walk, I'm not alone
My guardian Angels guide me along
And in my lonely hours of need
They hold me up and comfort me
They breathe life back in to my soul
Heal my heart and make it whole
I miss you in my life each day
Know that God's light shines my way….

I'd had a dream when I was still dating Walter the prior year of a tall slender man with sad blue eyes behind his glasses.

"He was standing in front of an old building. I came upon him as I walked out of the woods where I had wandered. He just looked at me with a sad smile upon his face. I kept thinking who is he?"

My Angels were talking again.

I did not meet him until my mother's family reunion in July of 2013. We knew each other as kids. My brother had invited him. He knew my family well and had worked for years for my stepfather at his cabinet shop. During the time, I had the dream in 2012 he was going through his divorce. We had a date in August. We went up to the islands for the day. I had had so many happy times with daddy on the beaches throughout the islands. I was lonely so I called him and asked if he wanted to spend the day with me. It was during that day that the dream hit me. He was the guy in my dream. We only knew each other 6 months. He spent so much time at my place he just moved in. I do not remember a conversation about us living together or even being a couple. It just happened. I had no thought or emotion attached to us.

Then about 4 months of dating, I had another dream.

"I was walking on a path and there was a cabin in my way. My brother and he were sitting at a fire beside a lake and they were just talking, drinking and smoking pot. I asked them to help me move the cabin out of my way. No, they were busy was the reply. So, I walked around the cabin in my path. And started up this path into the woods, knowing I need to get to the end of the path through the trees. Because I know Walter is up there somewhere. I get to the top and there is the bay, but I am by myself and the bay is covered in fog. I turn around and start down the dark path. I see a Harley coming at me with a bright light blinding me. It zooms past me but I see a young version of Walter. As I walk this large black panther appears, she walks beside me as I go back down to the lake. This panther brought me comfort and strength during this dream. She kept me from being afraid. Knowing I do not want to go back to the lake."

Walter called me 3 weeks after the dream. We had the 3 days together. On the fourth day he told me he was involved with someone, and I told him to never contact me again. As for my childhood friend, I knew I would not make him happy or be happy myself, if he stayed with me. Nor did I want him to. He brought me comfort when I needed it and I helped him during his time of grief. I told him to leave 2 weeks after the dream.

My Angels showed me my path and the way around what was blocking me from moving forward and finding myself. And for some reason this time I did not feel the need to withdraw into myself. I no longer wanted to hide my poetry or my dreams that I have had.

Accept Me as I Am

Accept me as I am
For I will accept no less
Accept me with my broken wings
For They've helped me to live and breathe
Accept me with my broken heart
For it has loved and been torn apart
Accept me as I am no less
For as my wings heal
So will my heart....

Grasp

Grasp your happiness
Hold it tight
For it heals all
With love and light

Grasp your happiness
Let it in
Let the love and laughter begin

Grasp your happiness
When it is there
For it carries you through
When burdens you bare

Grasp your happiness
Hold it tight
For Angels bring us happiness
To see God's light

Angels Given

There are angels around us young and small
Angels around us wise and tall
Given to us through God's grace
To help us learn and carry on
When with burdens we are placed
Angels to hold us close to them
To give us strength and believe again

From the Tide

The Hand of God is by my side
The hand that pulls me from the tide
It pulls me up and rescues me
When all is lost and I cannot see
This unseen hand that I feel
Brings me peace as I heal.
This force of strength from within
The hand of God helping me love again

All during this period I had experiences that sometimes freaked me out. The Summer of 2015 I would come home and the attic crawl space doors are open the doors straight out. This happened 4 times that summer. I thought it was maybe the heat. But, it did not happen in the prior summers. Nor in the summer of 2016 that was just as hot.

Over the past few years I have had many experiences at home and in my hotel rooms where my sheets are being blown around me. I know and feel the being next to me, above me, trying to get my attention. Other times I feel the wind all around me like I am laying in a wind tunnel and I can hear their chatter in my ears. One experience, I was sleeping and then I awaken and felt the weight of a body behind me hugging me from behind. There is also twice where I am on my right side and this dark body come up over from my back side and bends over me to looks in my face. I can see his cat like eyes and his yellow jagged teeth. I call to my Angels and I start the Lord prayers and repeat it over and over as I did as a child.

For I know these are not my Angels. What they want to tell me or want from me I do not know. Maybe because they know I hear my angels they want me to hear them. What I do know is that they are there. I now ask as I go to sleep of my angels, that if someone wants to come near me that they take my angels hands and they will take them where they need in to God's light. When my angels are near there is not fear, just knowledge that they are by me.

Just recently I heard my grandfather at about 6:00AM as I was just waking. "Well isn't that something" It was from in front of the China hutch he'd made for my grandmother when I was just a little girl. He gave it to her for a Christmas present. I was gifted it from my aunt who was moving to a retirement center. It holds many items and pictures of my parents, grandparents and great grandparents. On both my father and mother sides. I am glad grandpa likes where I have placed it.

In June of 2014 I had a dream of another man.

"He was in Scrubs, a face mask over his mouth and nose. I can see his clear blue eyes. He is in front of a drafting table and showing two women a blonde and a brunette on either side of him, blue prints. Next thing I know I am in a large vehicle. He is driving. I am in the passenger seat. I know that there are these two women behind us in the shadows of the back seat. It is pitch black outside. Between us is a huge console and I open it. There are dozens of tree roots tangled together. But from these roots, little leaves that are sparkling and glowing are growing. Twinkling emerald green and gold little leaves that keep multiplying. Hundreds of these little twinkling leaves."

During August 2014 I accept a date to meet a man over in the "Harbor". I knew his eyes when I met him. I had already seen them. He told me his name and I was shocked. He and my brother-in-law have the same first and middle name. He works at a hospital and builds homes when he is not at the hospital. Has two adult daughters a blonde and a brunette. And he drives a huge truck with an extended cab and the world biggest console between the driver seat and passenger seat. We sat in the late summer eve, drank wine and talked for a few hours. We walked together around the harbor. I drove home that night and literally heard daddy's chuckle from the back seat of my vehicle.

He was going through a tough period in his life this past winter of 2015. Not sure what was going to happen and where he was headed.

I had a dream again.

"We were swimming in a beautiful clear lake side by side. Then the lake turns to murky water, we are swimming around dead tree stumps. All the foliage on the trees that surround the lake is dead and the ground is muddy. I no longer wanted to be in the water. He keeps swimming in the murky mess. I walk out of the lake and call to him over my shoulder "I'll meet you at the cabin" I then climb a path up to a cabin on the hill above overlooking the lake"

Three days later I receive a text message from him of a cabin overlooking a lake. He'd written "where I want to live" It was the cabin and lake in my dream. Angels talking again.

I do not know where this path will lead or end. What I do know is I trust in myself again.

As for my family, I am blessed and thankful each day for my Son and Daughter. My son lives in Manhattan with his partner. I am so proud of my son and his passion to speak out. He lives life on his terms, gregariously with excitement and joy. My daughter is married. She amazes me with her determination help and love those around her. I am a Grandma now of a beautiful little blonde boy. He is my buddy, my Peanut. And I love watching my daughter learn motherhood with this little guy teaching her every step of the way.

I do not know what tomorrow brings. But I do know my angels will be there to guide me no matter which path I chose to go down. I listen intently and accept the messages they give me with gratitude and love.

The poetry flows from my pen and I receive it as I always have. It flows like a gift on to the pages. I am blessed to be able to know and feel my Family of Angels.

Roots of life

Sparkling little roots of life
Twinkling in the dark of night
Growing in the dusk of morn
Stretching tall all day long
Strengthening my resolve
To live my life from this day on...

Tangled Roots

Tangled roots revealed to me
Tangled roots of my dreams
And from these roots of my soul
Little green leaves that sparkled and glowed
Little green leaves in the darkness night
That grows from the tangled roots of life
Tangled roots revealed to me
Tangled roots of my dreams
In the dewy morning of the dawn
There is loveliness in the calm.

Miriam, Abram and Saul

Three angels of guidance sent to me
When my heavenly father heard my pleas
First was Miriam
Then came Saul
Abram then heard Gods loving call
My guardian angels next to me
Sent by God to comfort me
They offer guidance when I'm in need
They bring me hope when I stray
Miriam brings her motherly warmth
Her wings spread wide
Sheltering me from life storms
Saul offers comfort and hope
And helps me find ways to cope
And Abram brings a fathers' love
With wit, wisdom he guides me clear
My spirit guides one and all
Miriam, Abram, and Saul.

I hope my story of my journey to heal and find myself again gives others the knowledge and the strength to keep moving forward. You are not alone even in your darkest hours. I turned inward. Looked deep inside and started to listen quietly. And in doing so I opened my heart and mind back up to my heavenly father. I prayed so I would not be alone in this daily struggle to keep moving forward. I asked in tears night after night for his help. In doing so I was rewarded with reconnecting to the little girl inside who heard as a child, her angels. I survived Domestic Violence, I slayed a Monster that threatened to take me down into depths of a daily struggle with evil. I overcame, I have my children, living in the light of day with laughter and joy. I have their love and respect. Will we sometimes have triggers or falter? Yes, but they have learned that our love for each other was too strong to let what we had been through pull us apart.

I have learned to trust in myself, in the messages that God and my Family of Angels send to me. In this I find joy and inner peace.

***I was blessed after my Grandma passed away
with a dream of my family of Angels.***

I see a river that is flowing through a small valley. A path leads to the river. On the other side of the river is a white rail fence with a six-foot gap in it. There is not a bridge to the other side. The river is shallow with the water gently flowing over the rocks. Across the river I see a small valley with gentle sloping pastures. Surrounded by lush evergreen trees, spruce, cedars and firs, intermixed are alders, maples, cottonwoods covering the mountain slopes that surround the valley. Just beyond the fence are picnic tables with white and red checkered table clothes. The edges gently lift as the breeze flows through this valley. At the gate is Edythe, Wilma, Belle, Elsie, Jesse my grandmothers and great grandmothers, welcoming my family as they enter. All these ladies are hugging those who wade across the river. Edythe beckons those on the other side to cross the river as there is plenty of nourishment and love for all. Wilma sits quietly with her eyes twinkling, as her warm smile welcomes those who cross. There are others, sitting and mingling amongst the tables. Talking and sharing the food that has been prepared. Many are people I have known in life or seen in pictures of my ancestors and others I do not know. Merton my grandpa is blessing the food in his slow gentle way. Making sure the meat is carved and all are served. Grandpa John is out in the field with his dogs, cats and other animals surrounding him. He has his fedora in his hand and he is tossing a ball for a little gold cocker spaniel. My daddy J.A. is walking in from the forest with his fishing pole in one hand, rifle on his back. His hair is dark brown and full, his wide smile lights up his face. I can hear the chatter as they talk, laugh and gather together. The sky is clear blue, I can hear the trickle of the water, the birds chirping in the trees, the buzz of bees. I know when I pass that they will be there in this beautiful valley beckoning me to cross over the river. They will not let me falter.

Printed in the United States
By Bookmasters